THE DISCOVERY OF WITCHES

IN Answer to severall QUERIES, LATELY
Delivered to the Judges of Assize for the
County of NORFOLK

And now published by

MATTHEW HOPKINS, Witch-finder

FOR the Benefit of the whole KINGDOME

M. DC. XLVII.

EXOD. 22.18.

Thou shalt not suffer a witch to live.

Certaine *Queries* answered, which have been and are likely to be objected against MATTHEW HOPKINS, in his way of finding out *Witches*.

Querie 1.

That he must needs be the greatest Witch, Sorcerer, and Wizzard himselfe, else hee could not doe it.

Answ.

If Satan's kingdome be divided against it selfe, how shall it stand?

Querie 2.

If he never went so farre as is before mentioned, yet for certaine he met with the Devill, and cheated him of his Booke, wherein were written all the Witches names in England, and if he looks on any Witch, he can tell by her countenance what she is; so by this, his helpe is from the Devill.

Answ.

If he had been too hard for the devill and got his book, it had been to his great commendation, and no disgrace at all: and for judgement in *Phisiognomie*, he hath no more then any man else whatsoever.

Quer. 3.

From whence then proceeded this his skill? was it from his profound learning, or from much reading of learned Authors concerning that subject?

Answ.

From neither of both, but from experience, which though it be meanly esteemed of, yet the surest and safest way to judge by.

Quer. 4.

I pray where was this experience gained?
and why gained by him and not by others?

Answ.

The Discoverer never travelled far for it, but
in *March* 1644 he had some seven or eight
of that horrible sect of Witches living in the
Towne where he lived, a Towne in Essex
called *Maningtree*, with divers other
adjacent Witches of other towns, who every
six weeks in the night (being alwayes on the
Friday night) had their meeting close by his
house and had their severall solemne
sacrifices there offered to the *Devill*, one of
which this discoverer heard speaking to her
Imps one night, and bid them goe to another
Witch, who was thereupon apprehended,
and searched, by women who had for many
yeares knowne the Devills marks, and found
to have three teats about her, which honest
women have not: so upon command from
the *Justice* they were to keep her from sleep
two or three nights, expecting in that time to
see her *familiars*, which the fourth night she
called in by their severall names, and told
them what shapes, a quarter of an houre

before they came in, there being ten of us in the roome, the first she called was

1. *Holt*, who came in like a white kitling.

2. *Jarmara*, who came in like a fat Spaniel without any legs at all, she said she kept him fat, for she clapt her hand on her belly and said he suckt good blood from her body.

3. *Vinegar Tom*, who was like a long-legg'd Greyhound, with an head like an Oxe, with a long taile and broad eyes, who when this discoverer spoke to, and bade him goe to the place provided for him and his Angels, immediately transformed himselfe into the shape of a child of foure yeeres old without a head, and gave halfe a dozen turnes about the house, and vanished at the doore.

4. *Sack and Sugar*, like a black Rabbet.

5. *Newes*, like a Polcat. All these vanished away in a little time. Immediately after this Witch confessed severall other Witches, from whom she had her *Imps*, and named to divers women where their marks were, the number of their *Marks*, and *Imps*, and *Imps* names, as *Elemanzer*, *Pyewacket*, *Peckin the Crown*, *Grizzel*, *Greedigut*, &c. which no mortall could invent; and upon their searches the same Markes were found, the same number, and in the same place, and the like confessions from them of the same Imps, (though they knew not that we were told before) and so peached one another thereabouts that joyned together in the like damnable practise that in our Hundred in *Essex*, 29. were condemned at once, 4. brought 25. Miles to be hanged, where this Discoverer lives, for sending the Devill like a Beare to kill him in his garden, so by seeing diverse of the mens Papps, and trying wayes with hundreds of them, he gained this experience, and for ought he knowes any man else may find them as well as he and his company, if they had the same skill and experience.

Quer. 5.

Many poore People are condemned for having a Pap, or Teat about them, whereas many People (especially antient People) are, and have been a long time troubled with naturall wretts on severall parts of their bodies and other naturall excressencies, as Hemerodes, Piles, Childbearing, &c. and these shall be judged only by one man alone and a woman, and so accused or acquitted.

Answ.

The parties so judging can justifie their skill to any, and shew good reasons why such markes are not meerly naturall, neither that they can happen by any such naturall cause as is before expressed, and for further answer for their private judgements alone, it is most false and untrue, for never was any man tryed by search of his body, but commonly a dozen of the ablest men in the parish or else where, were present, and most commonly as many ancient skilfull matrons and midwives present when the women are tryed, which marks not only he, and his company attest to be very suspitious, but all beholders, the skilfulest of them, doe not approve of them, but likewise assent that such tokens cannot in their judgements proceed from any the above mentioned Causes.

Quer. 6.

It is a thing impossible for any or woman to judge rightly on such marks, they are so neare to naturall excressencies and they that finde them, durst not presently give Oath they were drawne by evil spirits, till they have used unlawfull courses of torture to make them say any thing for ease and quiet, as who would not do? but I would know the reasons he speakes of, how, and whereby to discover the one from the other, and so be satisfied in that.

Answ.

The reasons in breefe are three, which for the present he judgeth to differ from naturall marks which are:

1. He judgeth by the unusualnes of the place where he findeth the teats in or on their bodies being farre distant from any usuall place, from whence such naturall markes proceed, as if a witch plead the markes found are Emerods, if I finde them on the bottome of the back-bone, shall I assent with him, knowing they are not neere that veine, and so others by child-bearing, when it may be they are in the contrary part?

2. They are most commonly insensible, and feele neither pin, needle, aule, &c. thrust through them.

3. The often variations and mutations of these marks into severall formes, confirmes the matter; as if a Witch hear a month or two before that the Witch-finder (as they call him) is comming they will, and have put out their Imps to others to suckle them, even to their owne young and tender children; these upon search are found to have dry skinnes and filmes only, and be close to the flesh, keepe her 24. houres with a diligent eye, that none of her Spirits come in any visible shape to suck her; the women have seen the next day after her Teats extended out to their former filling length, full of corruption ready to burst, and leaving her alone then one quarter of an houre, and let the women go up againe and shee will have them drawn by her Imps close againe: Probatum est. Now for answer to their tortures in its due place.

Quer. 7.

How can it possibly be that the Devill bring a spirit, and wants no nutriment or sustentation, should desire to suck any blood? and indeed as he is a spirit he cannot draw any such excressences, having neither flesh nor bone, nor can be felt, &c.

Ans.

He seekes not their bloud, as if he could not subsist without that nourishment, but he often repairs to them, and gets it, the more to aggravate the Witches damnation, and to put her in mind of her Covenant; and as he is a Spirit and Prince of the ayre, he appeares to them in any shape whatsoever, which shape is occasioned by him through joyning of condensed thickned aire together, and many times doth assume shapes of many creatures; but to create any thing he cannot do it, it is only proper to God: But in this case of drawing out of these Teats, he doth really enter into the body, reall, corporeall, substantiall creature, and forceth that Creature (he working in it) to his desired ends, and useth the organs of that body to

speake withall to make his compact up with
the Witches, be the creature Cat, Rat,
Mouse, &c.

Quer. 8.

When these Paps are fully discovered, yet
that will not serve sufficiently to convict
them, but they must be tortured and kept
from sleep two or three nights, to distract
them, and make them say any thing; which
is a way to tame a wilde Colt, or Hawke, &c.

Ans.

In the infancy of this discovery it was not
only thought fitting, but enjoyned in *Essex*
and *Suffolke* by the Magistrates, with this
intention only, because they being kept
awake would be more the active to cal their
imps in open view the sooner to their helpe,
which oftentimes have so happened; and
never or seldome did any Witch ever
complaine in the time of their keeping for
want of rest, but after they had beat their
heads together in the Goale; and after this
use was not allowed of by the judges and
other Magistrates, it was never since used,
which is a yeare and a halfe since, neither
were any kept from sleep by any order or
direction since; but peradventure their own
stubborne wills did not let them sleep,
though tendered and offered to them.

Quer. 9.

Beside that unreasonable watching, they
were extraordinarily walked, till their feet
were blistered, and so forced through that
cruelty to confesse, &c.

Ans.

It was in the same beginning of this
discovery, and the meaning of walking of
them at the highest extent of cruelty, was
only they to walke about themselves the
night they were watched, only to keepe them
waking: and the reason was this, when they
did lye or sit in a chaire, if they did offer to
couch downe, then the watchers were only
to desire them to sit up and walke about, for
indeed when they be suffered so to couch,
immediately comes their Familiars into the
room and scareth the watchers, and
heartneth on the Witch, though contrary to
the true meaning of the same instructions,
diverse have been by rusticall People, (they
hearing them confess to be Witches) mis-
used, spoiled, and abused, diverse whereof
have suffered for the same, but could never
be proved against this Discoverer to have a

hand in it, or consent to it; and hath likewise been un-used by him and others, ever since the time they were kept from sleepe.

Quer. 10.

But there hath been an abominable, inhumane, and unmercifull tryall of these poore creatures, by tying them, and heaving them into the water; a tryall not allowable by Law or conscience, and I would faine know the reasons for that.

Ans.

It is not denyed but many were so served as had Papps, and floated, others that had none were tryed with them and sunk, but marke the reasons.

For first the Divels policie is great, in perswading many to come of their own accord to be tryed, perswading them their marks are so close they shall not be found out, so as diverse have come 10. or 12. Miles to be searched of their own accord, and hanged for their labour, (as one *Meggs* a

Baker did, who lived within 7. Miles of
Norwich, and was hanged at *Norwich*
Assizes for witchcraft) then when they find
that the Devil tells them false they reflect on
him, and he (as 40. have confessed) adviseth
them to be sworne, and tels them they shall
sinke and be cleared that way, then when
they be tryed that way and floate, they see
the Devill deceives them againe, and have so
laid open his treacheries.

2. It was never brought in against any of
them at their tryals as any evidence.

3. King *James* in his *Demonology* saith, it is
a certaine rule, for (saith he) Witches deny
their baptisme when they Covenant with the
Devill, water being the sole element thereof,
and therefore saith he, when they be heaved
into the water, the water refuseth to receive
them into her bosome, (they being such
Miscreants to deny their baptisme) and
suffers them to float, as the Froath on the
Sea, which the water will not recieve, but
casts it up and downe till it comes to the
earthy element the shore, and there leaves it

to consume.

4. Observe these generation of Witches, if they be at any time abused by being called Whore, Theefe, &c, by any where they live, they are the readiest to cry and wring their hands, and shed tears in abundance & run with full and right sorrowfull acclamations to some Justice of the Peace, and with many teares make their complaints: but now behold their stupidity; nature or the elements reflection from them, when they are accused for this horrible and damnable sin of Witchcraft, they never alter or change their countenances nor let one Teare fall. This by the way, swimming (by able Divines whom I reverence) is condemned for no way, and therefore of late hath, and for ever shall be left.

Quer. 11.

Oh! but if this torturing Witch-catcher can
by all or any of these meanes wring out a
word or two of confession from any of these
stupified, ignorant, unitelligible, poore silly
creatures, (though none heare it but
himselfe) he will adde and put her in feare to
confesse telling her, else she shall be
hanged; but if she doe, he will set her at
liberty, and so put a word into her mouth,
and make such a silly creature confesse she
knowes not what.

Answ.

He is of a better conscience, and for your
better understanding of him, he doth thus
uncase himselfe to all, add declares what
confessions (though made by a Witch
against her selfe) he allowes not of, and doth
altogether account of no validity, or worthy
of credence to be given to it, and ever did so
account it, and ever likewise shall.

1. He utterly denyes that confession of a Witch to be of any validity, when it is drawn from her by any torture or violence whatsoever; although after watching, walking, or swimming, diverse have suffered, yet peradventure Magistrates with much care and diligence did solely and fully examine them after sleepe, and consideration sufficient.

2. He utterly denyes that confession of a Witch, which is drawn from her by flattery, viz. if you will confess you shall go home, you shall not go to the Goale, nor be hanged, &c.

3. He utterly denyes that confession of a Witch, when she confesseth any improbability, impossibility, as flying in the ayre, riding on a broom, &c.

4. He utterly denyes a confession of a Witch, when it is interrogated to her, and words put into her mouth, to be of any force or effect: as to say to a silly (yet Witch wicked

enough) you have foure Imps have you not?
She answers affirmatively, Yes: did they not
suck you? Yes, saith she: Are not their
names so, and so? Yes, saith shee; Did not
you send such an Impe to kill my child? Yes
saith she, this being all her confession after
this manner, it is by him accompted nothing,
and he earnestly doth desire that all
Magistrates and Jurors would a little more
then ever they did examine witnesses about
the interrogated confessions.

Quer. 12.

If all those confessions be denyed, I wonder
what he will make confession, for sure it is,
all these wayes have been used and took for
good confessions, and many have suffered
for them, and I know not what, he will then
make confession.

Answ.

Yes, in brief he will declare what confession
of a Witch is of validity and force in his
judgement, to hang a Witch: when a Witch
is first found with teats, then sequestred
from her house, which is onely to keep her
old associates from her, and so by good

counsell brought into a sad condition, by understanding of the horribleness of her sin, and the judgements threatned against her; and knowing the Devils malice and subtile circumventions, is brought to remorse and sorrow for complying with Satan so long, and disobeying Gods sacred Commands, doth then desire to unfold her mind with much bitterness, and then without any of the before-mentioned hard usages or questions put to her, doth of her owne accord declare what was the occasion of the Devils appearing to her, whether ignorance, pride, anger, malice, &c. was predominant over her, she doth then declare what speech they had, what likeness he was in, what voice be had, what familiars he sent her, what number of spirits, what names they had, what shape they were in, what imployment she set them about to severall persons in severall places, (unknowne to the hearers) all which mischiefes being proved to be done, at the same time she confessed to the same parties for the same cause, and all effected, is testimony enough again her for all her denyall.

Quest. 13.

How can any possibly beleeve that the

Devill and the Witch joyning together, should have such power, as the Witches confesse to kill such such a man, child, horse, cow, the like; if we beleeve they can doe what they will, then we derogate from Gods power, who for certaine limits the Devill and the Witch; and I cannot beleeve they have any power at all.

Answ.

God suffers the Devill many times to doe much hurt, and the devill doth play many times the deluder and impostor with these Witches, in perswading them that they are the cause of such and such a murder wrought by him with their consents, when and indeed neither he nor they had any hand in it, as thus: We must needs argue, he is of a long standing, above 6000. yeers, then he must needs be the best Scholar in all knowledges of arts and tongues, & so have the best skill in *Physicke*, judgment in *Physiognomie*, and knowledge of what disease is reigning or predominant in this or that mans body, (and so for cattell too) by reason of his long experience. This subtile tempter knowing such a man lyable to some sudden disease, (as by experience I have found) as *Plurisie*, *Imposthume*, &c. he resorts to divers Witches; if they know the man, and seek to make a difference between the Witches and the party, it may be by telling them he hath threatned to have them very shortly searched, and so hanged for Witches, then they all consult with *Satan* to save themselves, and *Satan* stands ready prepared, with a What will you have me doe for you, my deare and nearest children, covenanted and compacted with me in my hellish league, and sealed with your blood, my delicate firebrand-darlings.

[

Oh thou (say they) that at the first didst promise to save us thy servants from any of out deadly enemies discovery, and didst promise to avenge and flay all those, we pleased, that did offend us; Murther that wretch suddenly who threatens the down-fall of your loyall subjects. He then promiseth to effect it. Next newes is heard the partie is dead, he comes to the witch, and gets a world of reverence, credence and respect for his power and activeness, when and indeed the disease kills the party, not the Witch, nor the Devill, (onely the Devill knew that such a disease was predominant) and the witch aggravates her damnation by her familiarity and consent to the Devill, and so comes likewise in compass of the Lawes. This is Satans usuall impostring and deluding, but not his constant course of proceeding, for he and the witch doe mischiefe too much. But I would that Magistrates and Jurats would a little examine witnesses when they heare witches confess such and such a murder, whether the party had not long time before, or at the time when the witch grew suspected, some disease or other predominant, which might cause that issue or effect of death.

Quer. 14.

All that the witch-finder doth is to fleece the country of their money, and therefore rides and goes to townes to have imployment, and promiseth them faire promises, and it may be doth nothing for it, and possesseth many men that they have so many wizzards and so many witches in their towne, and so hartens them on to entertaine him.

Ans.

You doe him a great deale of wrong in every of these particulars. For, first,

1. He never went to any towne or place, but they rode, writ, or sent often for him, and were (for ought he knew) glad of him.

2. He is a man that doth disclaime that ever he detected a witch, or said, Thou art a witch; only after her tryall by search, and their owne confessions, he as others may judge.

3. Lastly, judge how he fleeceth the Country, and inriches himselfe, by considering the vast summe he takes of every towne, he demands but 20.s. a town, & doth sometimes ride 20. miles for that, & hath no more for all his charges thither and back again (& it may be stayes a weeke there) and finde there 3. or 4. witches, or if it be but one, cheap enough, and this is the great summe he takes to maintaine his

Companie with 3. horses.

Judicet ullus.

Printed in Great Britain
by Amazon

10512425R00018